Sammie Crawford

Photography by **Harry Crawford**

Schiffer Publishing Ltd

4880 Lower Valley Road • Atglen, PA • 19310

Other Schiffer Books by Sammie Crawford:
Gourd Fun for Everyone, 978-0-7643-3124-4, $22.99
Holiday Fun: Painting Christmas Gourds, 978-0-7643-3279-1, $14.99
Building Gourd Birdhouses with the Fairy Gourdmother, 978-0-7643-3736-9, $24.99

Other Schiffer Books on Related Subjects:
Apples to Apples: Basic Techniques for Decorating Gourds, 978-0-7643-3621-8, $19.99
Gourd Crafts: 6 Projects & Patterns, 978-0-7643-2825-1, $14.95
Decorating Gourds: Carving, Burning, Painting, and More, 0-7643-1312-6, $14.95

Designed by Danielle D. Farmer
Cover Design by Bruce Waters
Type set in Zapfino/Arrus BT/Humanist521 BT

ISBN: 978-0-7643-3735-2
Printed in China

PUBLISHING

Schiffer Books are available at special discounts for bulk purchases for sales promotions or premiums. Special editions, including personalized covers, corporate imprints, and excerpts can be created in large quantities for special needs. For more information contact the publisher:

Published by Schiffer Publishing Ltd.
4880 Lower Valley Road
Atglen, PA 19310

Phone: (610) 593-1777; Fax: (610) 593-2002
E-mail: Info@schifferbooks.com

For the largest selection of fine reference books on this and related subjects, please visit our web site at: **www.schifferbooks.com**

We are always looking for people to write books on new and related subjects. If you have an idea for a book please contact us at the above address.

This book may be purchased from the publisher.
Include $5.00 for shipping.
Please try your bookstore first.
You may write for a free catalog.

In Europe, Schiffer books are distributed by
Bushwood Books
6 Marksbury Ave.
Kew Gardens
Surrey TW9 4JF England

Phone: 44 (0) 20 8392 8585; Fax: 44 (0) 20 8392 9876
E-mail: info@bushwoodbooks.co.uk
Website: **www.bushwoodbooks.co.uk**

ACKNOWLEDGMENTS

Thanks to Schiffer's senior editor, Doug Congdon-Martin, for being so helpful and making this such a fun project. I also want to thank my husband for all he does, from serving as my photographer to putting up with hundreds of gourds in every nook and crannie of his shop. And I can't forget to thank the Supreme Gourdwasher, 92-year-old Betty Torgerson — without her, I'd still be scrubbing gourds instead of painting them.

This book is dedicated to animal lovers everywhere and especially to the bird lovers among you. My three little companions — Rascal, Lil' Bit, and Minnie P. Barker — remind me to enjoy all the little things life offers. Fun is where you find it and for me it's in every gourd I pick up. May you all have as much fun building and painting these birds as I did.

CONTENTS

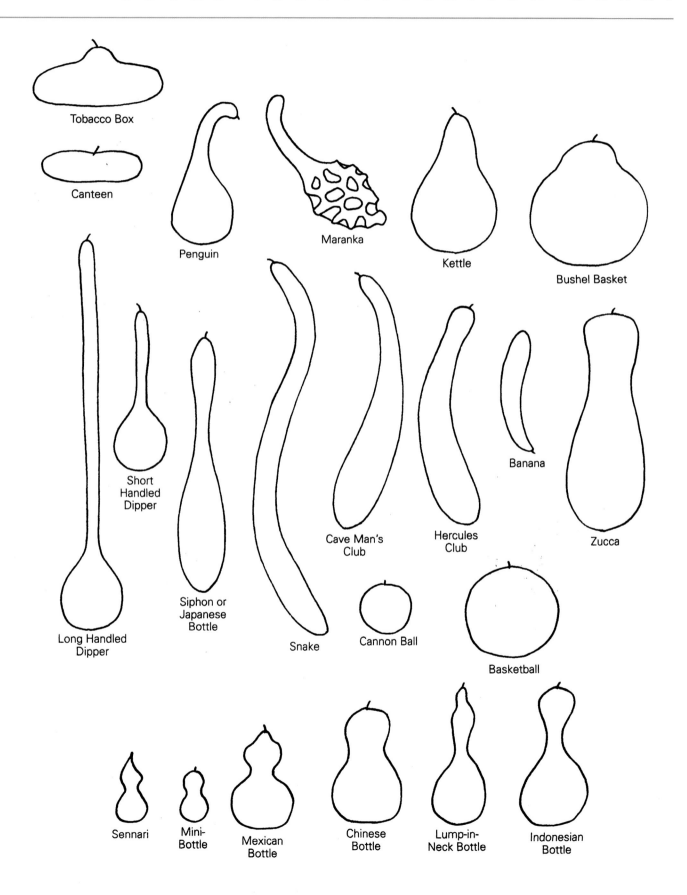

Tobacco Box

Canteen

Penguin

Maranka

Kettle

Bushel Basket

Short Handled Dipper

Siphon or Japanese Bottle

Cave Man's Club

Hercules Club

Banana

Zucca

Long Handled Dipper

Snake

Cannon Ball

Basketball

Sennari

Mini-Bottle

Mexican Bottle

Chinese Bottle

Lump-in-Neck Bottle

Indonesian Bottle

GETTING STARTED

Harvesting the Gourd

If you are growing your own gourds and this is your first time, be sure to wait until the first frost before harvesting them. If you pick them before the vine has dried and the stems have turned brown, there is a better chance that the gourds will rot rather than dry.

Once harvested, you must find a place where the sun and air can get to them. Fortunately, I have a place where I make a chicken-wire hammock for them and the air can circulate around them really well. Any place will do as long as they are up off the ground, even on a wooden pallet.

They can even be left on the vine through the winter. The only drawback is if you intend to use the seeds and they freeze, they won't germinate as well as seeds that haven't frozen, but they will grow.

When they start to dry, they will turn black and moldy. Don't throw them away! This is where first-time growers panic, thinking that they are ruined. This is just part of the drying process. Since they are ninety percent water, all that moisture must evaporate through the skin and as long as there are no soft spots in them, you are okay. When they are dry, they will be very lightweight and usually the seeds will rattle inside.

Cleaning the Gourd

Once the gourds are dry, it's time to remove all the mold and dried skin from the gourd.

First, place it in the sink with several inches of warm water and about 1/4 cup of bleach. Let the gourd soak for five to ten minutes, turning it to wet all the sides. Use a plastic scrubber (I prefer Dobie pads) to scrub off the softened mold. If some spots are stubborn, use a dull paring knife to scrape it because if you don't remove every bit of mold it can loosen later and take your paint with it when if falls off.

When the gourd is clean, let it dry overnight or, if you're in a hurry, place it in the oven at 225 degrees for ten minutes. Now you're ready to paint. There is no need to use sealer — you gotta love that!

What to do Before Painting

Every gourd is different and because they're different, each pattern in this book will require some sort of adjustment — whether it's enlarging or reducing it to fit your particular gourd. The best way to apply a flat pattern to a round surface is to cut the pattern tracing into pieces and then applying the individual features where needed.

VARNISHING

Varnishing instructions are the same on each project. When spraying, always allow drying time between coats of varnish. Several light coats are always better than one heavy one because heavy spray can run and ruin your piece. You've spent way too much time making this beautiful piece to get in a hurry now.

SANDING

When sanding the spackle, start with medium grit sandpaper like a 150 and then finish with a finer grit like 600. This gives a smooth satin finish and makes your joints undetectable.

After applying the spackle, dampen your fingers to smooth the edges. Don't use too much water or it will remove the spackle just as too little will. You'll know when you have it right — and don't try to get it perfectly smooth. Sanding will take care of any ridges. Better to apply too much spackle and sand off the excess than to apply too little.

As a rule, it's better to sand across the spackle ridges to avoid deepening the valleys between them.

GLUING

A thick layer of wood glue applied to the back of a thin gourd will add strength after drying overnight. The self-leveling glue will also give you a smoother surface to paint. Once the glue dries, you can fill any remaining holes with spackle, then sand, and the inside should be as smooth as the outside.

When adding gourd pieces such as wings to another gourd, try to pick a gourd whose curves match as closely as possible those of the gourd being added to. Not only does this give more surface for gluing, but the pieces are not as likely to be knocked off or broken if they hug the surface of the other gourd.

Your "usual painting supplies" should include tracing paper, transfer paper in black and white, palette paper, a divided water tub or two water containers, Q-tips®, a good grade paper towels, stylus, palette knife, short flexible ruler, kneaded eraser, sponge, pencil and charcoal, and chalk pencils.

In addition, I usually keep a bottle of blending gel in my tote. Keeping these things stocked in a divided plastic tote makes it easier to pack when going places like classes, demonstrations, and craft shows. You only have to add the brushes and paints you'll need and you're ready to go.

Terminology

Don't be confused by the terms used here. These are some of the most common terms and their definitions:

Float, shade, and sideload:

These all mean the same thing. This is when you load paint onto the corner of your brush and blend it to paint a shadow or highlight.

Retarder, extender, and blending gel:

Three more words that are the same — this is just a medium used to give you a longer open time, to extend the drying time so you can work the paint longer.

Wash:

This is 90% water and 10% paint and is used to soften when your shade or highlight may be too stark. The wash helps unite the base, shadows, and highlights.

Painting Stroke Illustrations

In each of the following three stroke illustrations, you will be using water to thin paint. This is the only time you will add water to your paints for the projects in this book.

Painting Stroke Illustrations

Floating or Side-loading a Brush

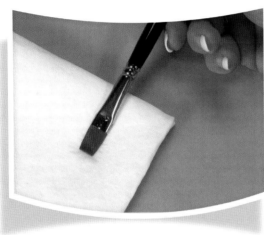

Use at least a #12 or 1/2" wide brush. Moisten the brush with clean water and blot on a paper towel just until it loses its sheen. Leave as much water without it being drippy.

Holding it at a 45-degree angle, dip the corner of the brush in the paint.

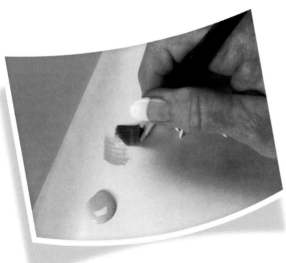

Apply a slight pressure and work the brush back and forth on the palette. Be careful not to let the paint get on the clean side of the brush.

Flip the brush over and gently pinch off the water from the brush. Some people don't do this, but I find I have a "halo" along the edge of my float if I don't.

Painting Stroke Illustrations

Using a Liner Brush

When using a liner brush, always thin the paint to the consistency of milk or ink. Do this by pulling a small amount of paint over to a drop of water on your palette. (If you don't thin it, the paint will not flow off the brush tip.)

When the brush is dressed, pull the point back in shape by rotating the brush between your fingers as you pull it across the palette. Regular liners are fine for comma strokes, but if you are making long lines, try using a script liner.

Using Your Rake Brush

Moisten your brush and blot on a paper towel just until it loses its shine. Dress the brush with paint and work it back and forth on the palette. Set the brush down on the palette and fan the bristles by applying slight pressure and rotating the brush between your fingers. But don't let the metal ferrule touch because it can cut the bristles off.

If you have the correct amount of water and paint in your brush, light strokes will produce fine lines. Too much or too little water and it makes a solid stroke. It's just a matter of practice. Once you find the balance, you will really enjoy making hair, beards, and fur.

H O W   T O   F L O A T . . .

There is more than one way to float. If you are having difficulty getting a nice, smooth float, try one of these methods.

1. Moisten the surface with water before floating. Don't flood it, just dampen it.

2. If that doesn't do it, try blending gel. Use a separate brush to paint the area with blending gel before floating then float as usual.

3. If these two methods don't yield the desired result, try double loading your brush. Dress the entire brush in your base color then dip the corner in the color you're floating with. Work the brush back and forth to blend the two colors just as you would for a regular float and paint.

. . . & O T H E R   U S E F U L   T I P S

- Close your eyes and run your fingers over the piece when you are doing that final sanding. You will feel things your eyes missed and you'll get a much smoother finish.

- Keep a dampened cotton swab handy for an eraser. Go ahead and dampen and squeeze dry both ends because when you need it, you don't have time to figure out which end is wet.

- When sponging, turn your sponge frequently to avoid a "cookie cutter" look unless you are going for a specific pattern.

- Always use your mop brush dry. To remove excess paint during a process, rub the brush in a circular motion on a damp spot of your paper towel. Only wash it completely when you are finished with it.

Here are some basic instructions for making a plywood bottom. Though only the "Penguin & Chick" project, featured in this book, call for a bottom, any project could actually have one.

Place the gourd on the plywood and draw around it. Mark the gourd and the board so they can be matched up once the cut is made.

Allowing for the thickness of the gourd, draw a second line inside the first one. This will be your cutting line.

Make the cut. Notice the mark has been extended into the circle so it won't be lost when the circle is cut.

Mark the inside with an "X" and then extend the mark on the side to the other side of the wood.

Align the marks and try the piece for fit. It probably won't fit on the first try, so sand where needed until it does. Add any needed weight at this point. I use buckshot or kitty litter to add stability.

Spackle any cracks and sand smooth when dry. Paint as you would the rest of the gourd.

THE PROJECTS

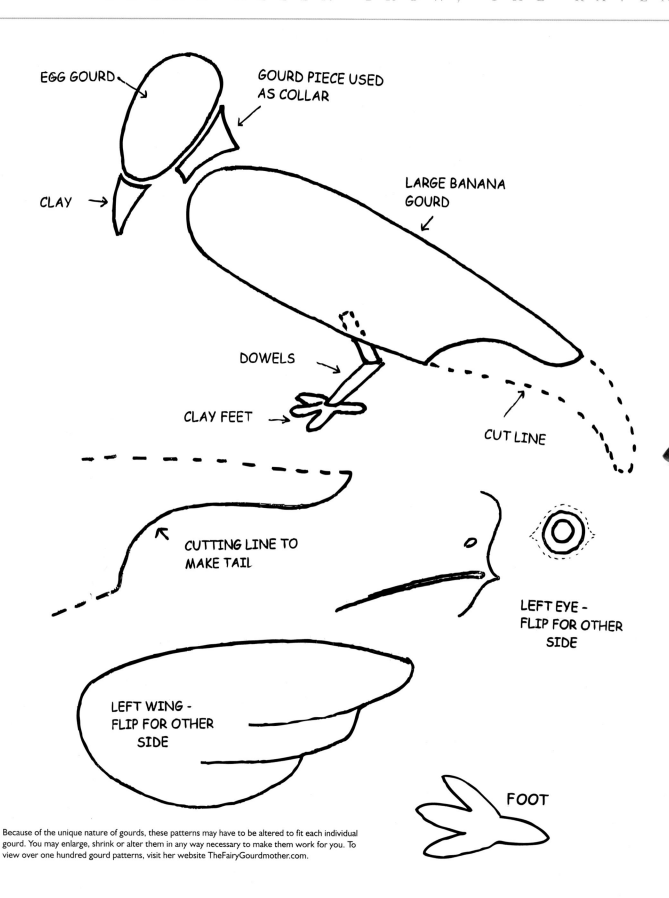

EGG GOURD

GOURD PIECE USED AS COLLAR

CLAY

LARGE BANANA GOURD

DOWELS

CLAY FEET

CUT LINE

CUTTING LINE TO MAKE TAIL

LEFT EYE - FLIP FOR OTHER SIDE

LEFT WING - FLIP FOR OTHER SIDE

FOOT

Because of the unique nature of gourds, these patterns may have to be altered to fit each individual gourd. You may enlarge, shrink or alter them in any way necessary to make them work for you. To view over one hundred gourd patterns, visit her website TheFairyGourdmother.com.

Edgar Allen Crow, the Raven

PALETTE

Black ~ White ~ Rain Grey ~ Storm Grey ~ Autumn Brown ~ Dark Goldenrod ~ Gleams Bobby Blue ~ Blue iridescent glaze

BRUSHES

Series 7120 1/2" rake ~ Series 7300 #12 flat ~ Series 7350 10/0 liner ~ Series 7500 #4 filbert ~ Series 7550 1" wash

SUPPLIES

Extra large banana gourd ~ Egg gourd ~ Gourd pieces ~ DAP Fast n' Final spackle ~ Fimo clay ~ Wood glue ~ 1/2" wooden dowel, 6" long ~ Craft saw ~ Fine grit sandpaper

Assembly

Apply the cutting pattern to the small end of a banana gourd and cut. Apply the wing pattern to a scrap gourd and cut two wings, remembering to reverse the pattern for the second wing. Cut a small section for the neck, per the diagram. The beak is cut from any gourd with a pointed end. Cut a piece of scrap to fill in at the back where you cut off for the tail.

Glue the beak on the egg gourd; glue the egg and neck piece onto the banana gourd. Glue in the scrap under the tail. It's best to paint the wings before gluing in place. Drill 1/2" holes for the dowel legs. Cut the dowels at an angle and then turn one piece 180 degrees and glue back together. When dry, glue the dowels in the holes.

Using Fimo clay, roll out a rope of conditioned clay and cut off eight equal pieces for the toes. Roll each piece out to 3/4" long, tapering the ends, and place on aluminum foil, according to the pattern. Use a dowel to make an indention where the toes join. This joins them and makes a place for the dowel later. Bake according to package directions.

Spackle all the joints. You may moisten your fingertips to smooth the joints before drying, but don't worry about getting it perfect. Sandpaper works wonders.

Painting the Piece

Use the wash brush to paint the entire bird Black except for the dowels. The beak is Storm Grey.

Use the rake brush to pull Black streaks on the beak. The nostrils are also Black.

Use the liner brush to paint a line of separation between the upper and lower beaks.

With the same brush and Rain Grey, outline the Black line. When dry, wash the beak with Black.

Use the #12 brush to float Bobby Blue on the edges of the wings and tail.

Use the filbert brush to base-coat the eye Autumn Brown.

Float Dark Goldenrod across the top of the eye.

Float Black across the bottom of the eye.

Paint the pupil Black.

Use the liner brush and White to place a comma stroke in the eye.

Use the #12 flat to float Storm Grey around the eye …

… leaving a small ring of Black next to the eye.

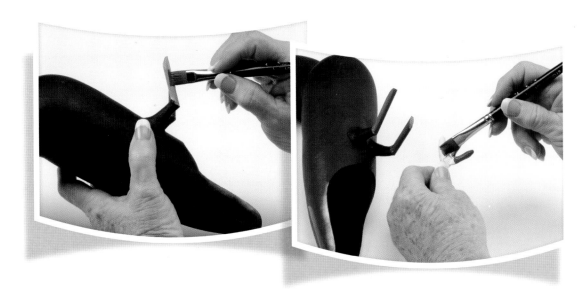

Paint the lower legs and feet Storm Grey.

Glaze the entire bird except the lower legs and feet with the iridescent glaze. No varnish is necessary.

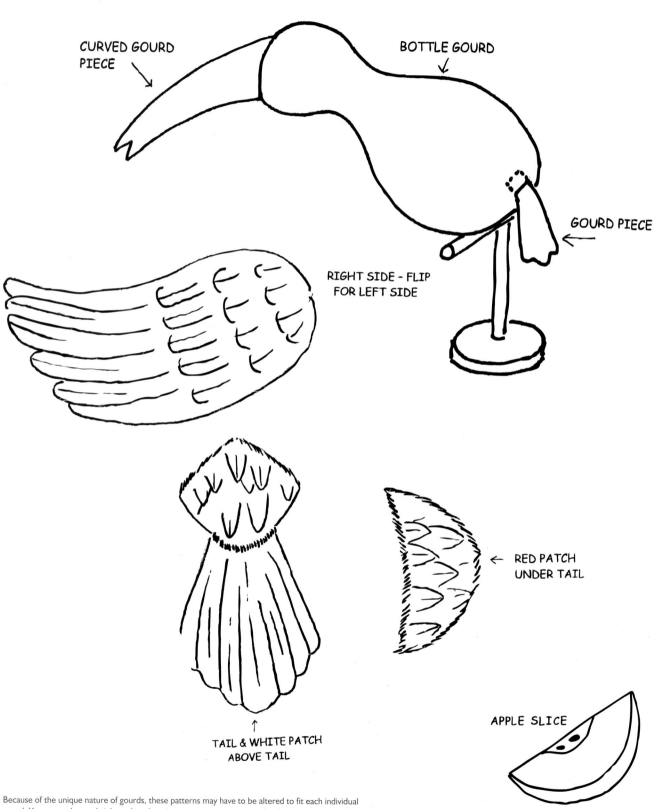

CURVED GOURD PIECE

BOTTLE GOURD

GOURD PIECE

RIGHT SIDE - FLIP FOR LEFT SIDE

RED PATCH UNDER TAIL

TAIL & WHITE PATCH ABOVE TAIL

APPLE SLICE

Because of the unique nature of gourds, these patterns may have to be altered to fit each individual gourd. You may enlarge, shrink or alter them in any way necessary to make them work for you. To view over one hundred gourd patterns, visit her website TheFairyGourdmother.com.

Toucan

PALETTE

Black ~ Opaque Red ~ Yellow ~ White ~ Pigskin ~ Custard ~ Quaker Grey ~ Blue Danube ~ Storm Grey ~ Roman Stucco ~ Gecko Green ~ Orange Pop ~ O.J. ~ Blue Mist ~ Lime Green ~ Black Cherry ~ Mocha ~ Light Ivory ~ Moroccan Red

BRUSHES

Series 7300 #12 flat ~ Series 7350 10/0 liner ~ Series 7520 1/2" rake filbert ~ Series 7550 1" wash brush

SUPPLIES

Round gourd 5-7" diameter ~ Large egg gourd ~ Scrap gourd pieces (slightly curved club) ~ Dowels for stand (see Macaw pattern) ~ Wood glue ~ DAP Fast n' Final spackle ~ Fine grit sandpaper ~ Craft saw

Assembly

Cut off a section of the curved club, fit snugly to the egg gourd (head), and glue. When dry, remove a small section of the egg gourd, fit to the round gourd (body), and glue. Cut a small "v" shape from the small end of the beak to separate the upper and lower sections. Apply the pattern to a piece of scrap and cut... Cut a slot in the rear of the body and fit the tail in place. Do not glue in place until the pieces are painted. (Do as I say, not as I did!)

Drill a hole where the feet will be, insert the inch-long 1/2" dowel half way and glue. Apply spackle to all the joints (except the tail) and sand smooth when dry.

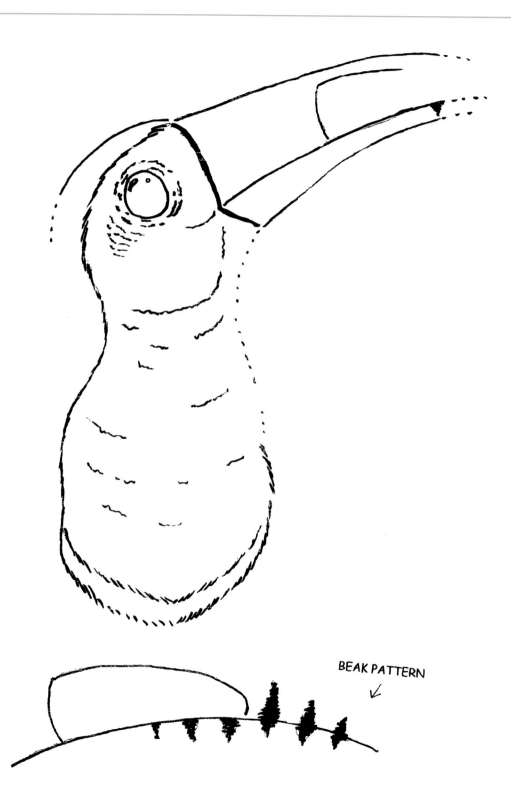

BEAK PATTERN

Because of the unique nature of gourds, these patterns may have to be altered to fit each individual gourd. You may enlarge, shrink or alter them in any way necessary to make them work for you. To view over one hundred gourd patterns, visit her website TheFairyGourdmother.com.

Painting the Piece

Basecoat the bird's body, back of his head and his tail Black except for the small patch of White above the tail and the patch of Opaque Red under the tail and the tip of the beak.

Basecoat the head, beak and breast Yellow. The line at the base of the beak and the eye are Black.

Use the rake brush and Opaque Red to make a tapered, jagged line around the bottom of the Yellow bib with the widest part in the center. Also use the rake brush anywhere two colors meet to avoid a solid line and keep it looking feathered.

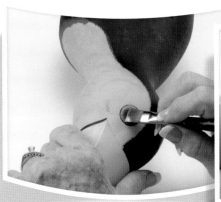  

Float Quaker Grey around the eye around the edges, leaving a tiny line of Black at the edge.

Place a White comma stroke and a couple of dots in the eye for highlight.

Use the #12 flat to float Blue Danube in circles around the eye using a "nervous" wiggly motion.

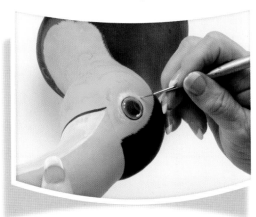

Use the liner brush to add a few lines within the floats.

Float Pigskin lines on the breast and under the cheek.

Highlight the cheek with Custard.

Float Storm Grey to highlight the feathers in the black section.

Shade around the feathers in the white section with the same color.

With the same color, use the liner brush to make the veins on all feathers.

Shade around the feathers in the red section with Black Cherry.

Paint the upper beak with Gecko Green and the lower beak with Blue Mist.

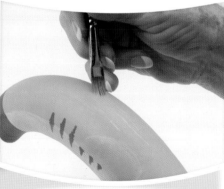

Use the rake brush to streak some Lime Green on the upper beak.

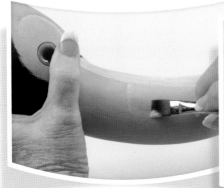

Paint the light section with O.J. and float around the edges with Orange Pop. The ragged markings are Storm Grey.

Paint the perch Roman Stucco. Paint the feet on the perch in Storm Grey.

Highlight with Quaker Grey and White 1:1.

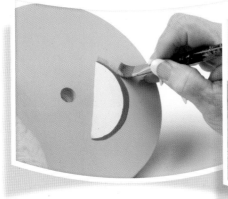

Shade around the feet with Mocha.

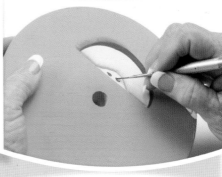

Paint the apple slice Light Ivory and the peel Moroccan Red. Using the #12 flat, shade around one edge of the apple with around the seed pit with Mocha and White 2:3.

Use the liner brush and Storm Grey to make the seeds. Glue the stand together and glue a nut in the bird's beak if you like. Finish with several light coats of spray varnish.

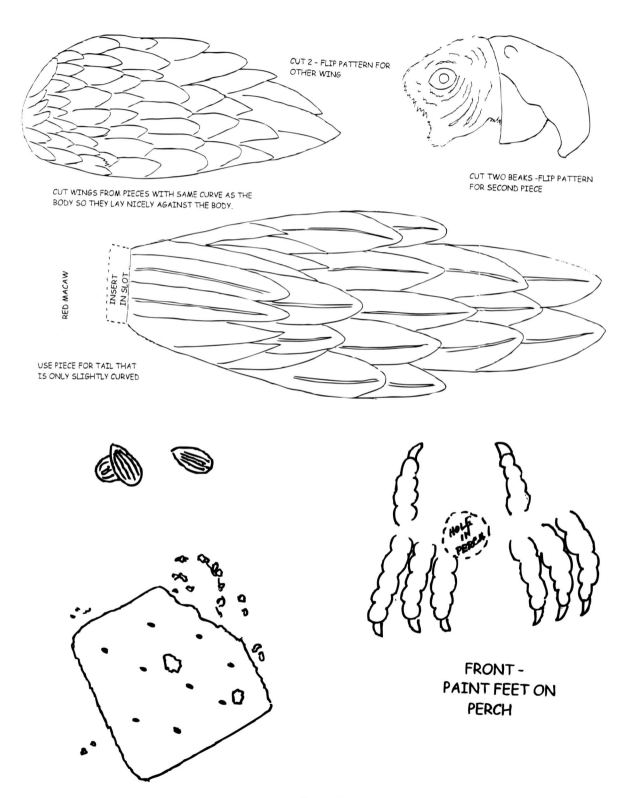

CUT 2 - FLIP PATTERN FOR
OTHER WING

CUT WINGS FROM PIECES WITH SAME CURVE AS THE
BODY SO THEY LAY NICELY AGAINST THE BODY.

CUT TWO BEAKS - FLIP PATTERN
FOR SECOND PIECE

RED MACAW

INSERT IN SLOT

USE PIECE FOR TAIL THAT
IS ONLY SLIGHTLY CURVED

HOLE IN PERCH

FRONT -
PAINT FEET ON
PERCH

PAINT ON BASE

Because of the unique nature of gourds, these patterns may have to be altered to fit each individual
gourd. You may enlarge, shrink or alter them in any way necessary to make them work for you. To
view over one hundred gourd patterns, visit her website TheFairyGourdmother.com.

Red Macaw

PALETTE

Opaque Red ~ White ~ Cricket ~ Poppy Orange ~ Black Cherry ~ Tangerine ~ Ocean Reef ~ Blue Danube ~ Navy Blue ~ Opaque Yellow ~ Antique Gold ~ Pale Yellow ~ Raw Sienna ~ Light Timberline ~ Apple Green ~ Burnt Sienna ~ Hunter Green ~ Drizzle Grey ~ Black ~ Rain Grey ~ Mello Yellow ~ Chocolate Cherry ~ Toffee ~ Light Ivory

BRUSHES

Series 7300 #12 flat ~ Series 7350 10/0 liner ~ Series 7500 #6 filbert ~ Series 7520 1/2" filbert rake ~ Series 7550 1" wash brush

SUPPLIES

Bottle gourd, 10" tall ~ Gourd scraps ~ 6" dia. wooden circle ~ 1/2" dowel, 12" long ~ 1/2" dowel, 1" long ~ 1" dowel, 6" long ~ Wood glue ~ Satin spray varnish ~ Fimo clay and craft saw ~ 1/2" drill bit and drill

Assembly

Apply the pattern and cut the wings, beak, and tail from the gourd pieces. Glue the beak together. It is only going to come together on one plane. Use the Fimo clay to fill in the gaps and bake according to package directions. Glue the beak and tail in place. Fill the area where the tail and body meet with spackle and allow to dry overnight. Sand smooth.

If desired, you may fill this area with Fimo clay instead of spackle and bake. The heat will not harm the gourds. Do not glue the wings on yet.

Drill a hole in the bottom of the gourd and glue the 1" long gourd half way in.

THE STAND

Drill a hole all the way through the 6" long dowel and a matching hole in the round base. Glue the 12" long dowel into the round base. Insert the other end of the 12" dowel halfway through the 6" long dowel and glue. This leaves room for the dowel in the bottom of bird to fit in later.

Painting the Piece

Basecoat all red feathers with Opaque Red, all blue feathers in Ocean Blue, and all yellow feathers in Opaque Yellow. The beak bottom is Black and the top is a Light Ivory and Pale Yellow 1:8 mix. Use this same mix for the area around the eye. The perch is Hunter Green.

Use the wash brush and Poppy Orange to wash all red feathers.

Use the #12 flat and Black Cherry to shade around the feathers and down each side of the veins in the red areas.

Use the liner brush and Tangerine to highlight the veins. Use the #12 to highlight the feather tips.

Use the #12 sand Navy Blue to shade around the feathers and down each side of the veins in the blue areas.

Use the #12 flat and Blue Danube to highlight the blue feathers.

Use the liner brush and Blue Danube to paint the veins.

Use the #12 flat and Antique Gold to shade around the feathers and down each side of the veins.

Use the #12 flat and Pale Yellow to highlight the feather tips. Use the liner brush to paint the veins.

Use the liner and corresponding shading colors in each area to paint random "splits" in the feathers.

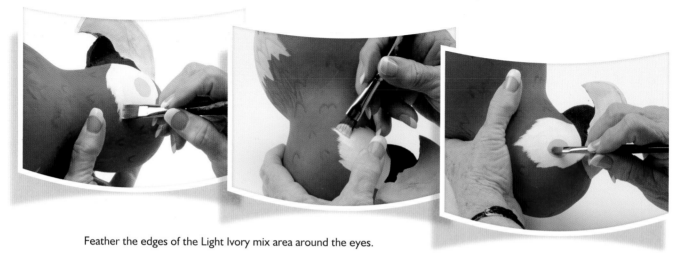

Feather the edges of the Light Ivory mix area around the eyes.

Use the filbert and paint the eyes with a Cricket & Light Timberline mix 4:1.

Paint ragged floats of Raw Sienna around the eyes.

Float Apple Green across the top of the eyes.

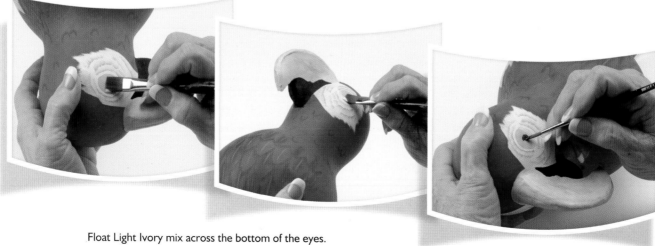

Float Light Ivory mix across the bottom of the eyes.

Paint the pupil Chocolate Cherry.

Using the liner brush, line the top of the eyes with Chocolate Cherry.

Line the bottom of the eyes with Burnt Sienna.

With White paint, use the liner brush to place a comma stroke in the eyes.

Tap in a touch of Blue Danube around the eyes and mop to soften.

Use the #12 flat and Antique Gold to float around the edges of the beak where it meets the head and the bottom beak.

Touch in a little Blue Danube near the base of the beak.

The nostrils are "c" strokes of Chocolate Cherry. Glue the wings in place and allow to dry for several hours or overnight.

The Toes

Paint the toes Rain Grey and shade with Black.

Highlight the toes with a mix of Rain Grey & White 1:1.

The Stand

Base the cracker and crumbs with the Light Ivory mix and the seeds with Drizzle Grey. Shade the cracker edges with Drizzle Grey.

Tap in Mello Yellow with the flat brush then quickly mop to soften.

Tap in a little Raw Sienna over some of the Mello Yellow and mop to soften.

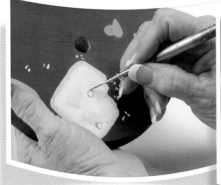

Use the liner brush and Toffee to line the holes.

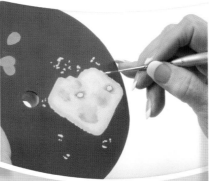

Touch White "bumps" to the edge of the cracker to make it look perforated.

Use the #12 flat to shade the black holes with Drizzle.

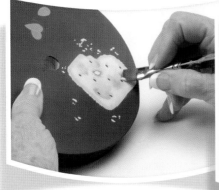

Use the #12 flat to shade the black holes with Drizzle.

Float a Black shadow on the perch around two sides of the cracker.

Use the liner brush to make the Rain Grey lines on the seeds.

Shade around and between the seeds with Black.

Lightly highlight the seeds with Light Ivory.

At this point, you may glue the bird to the perch or leave it loose for ease of transportation. Finish with several light coats of varnish.

FLIP PATTERN
FOR RIGHT SIDE

Because of the unique nature of gourds, these patterns may have to be altered to fit each individual gourd. You may enlarge, shrink or alter them in any way necessary to make them work for you. To view over one hundred gourd patterns, visit her website TheFairyGourdmother.com.

Penguin & Chick

PALETTE

Soft Grey ~ Rain Grey ~ Rouge ~ Bittersweet ~ Black ~ White

BRUSHES

Series 7300 #12 flat brush ~ Series 7350 10/0 liner brush ~ Series 7550 1" wash brush

SUPPLIES

8-10" penguin gourd ~ Large egg gourd ~ DAP Fast n' Final spackle ~ Gloss spray varnish ~ Silk sponge ~ Wood glue ~ Fimo clay ~ Craft saw ~ Scrap of 1/4" plywood ~ Buckshot or kitty litter (optional)

Assembly

Cut a hole in the egg gourd and slip the end of the penguin gourd into it to create the head. Glue in place and let dry 1-2 hours or overnight. Cut off the other end of the gourd and insert a plywood bottom (see instructions in Section One). Put a small amount of buckshot inside before gluing the bottom in place if it's needed to keep the bird upright.

Fill in where the two gourds join with spackle; smooth and sand when dry. Form the beak on the gourd with Fimo clay and place the entire gourd in the oven. Bake according to package directions.

Painting the Piece

Apply the pattern and use the wash brush to basecoat the Black and White portions.

Use the #12 flat and Rain Grey to float around the eyes. Float inside on the eye to make the eye appear round

Use the same brush and color to float around the flippers.

Float Bittersweet on the cheeks.

Use the liner brush and Bittersweet to place the line on the beak.

Use the liner brush and White to place a comma stroke in each eye for sparkle.

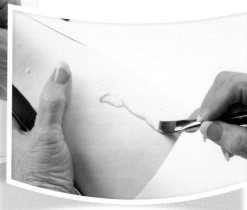

Use the #12 flat and Rain Grey to float the outline of the chick on the bird, fading toward the center.

2 | T H E   P R O J E C T S

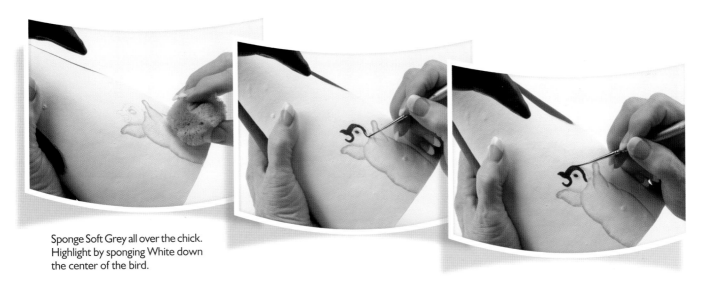

Sponge Soft Grey all over the chick.
Highlight by sponging White down
the center of the bird.

Use the liner brush and Black to paint the chick's head and eye.

Paint the tongue Rouge.

Place a White dot in the eyes, and finish
with several coats of spray varnish

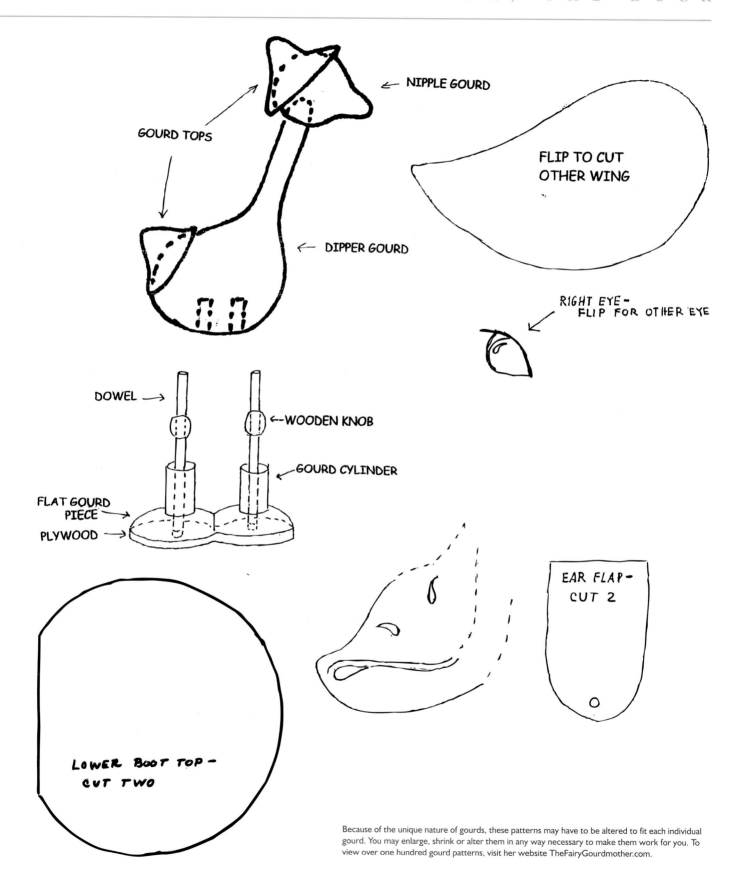

NIPPLE GOURD

GOURD TOPS

FLIP TO CUT
OTHER WING

DIPPER GOURD

RIGHT EYE -
FLIP FOR OTHER EYE

DOWEL →

←WOODEN KNOB

GOURD CYLINDER

FLAT GOURD
PIECE

PLYWOOD

EAR FLAP -
CUT 2

LOWER BOOT TOP -
CUT TWO

Because of the unique nature of gourds, these patterns may have to be altered to fit each individual
gourd. You may enlarge, shrink or alter them in any way necessary to make them work for you. To
view over one hundred gourd patterns, visit her website TheFairyGourdmother.com.

Affleck, the Duck

P A L E T T E

White ~ Green ~ Yellow ~ Black ~ Pigskin ~ Custard ~ Quaker Grey

B R U S H E S

Series 7300 #12 flat ~ Series7350 10/0 liner ~ Series 7500 #6 filbert ~ Series 7550 1" wash brush

S U P P L I E S

Dipper gourd ~ Nipple gourd ~ Gourd pieces ~ Watercolor paper ~ 2 1/2" dowels approx. 8" long ~ 2 wooden beads ~ Rattail ribbon ~ 1/2" drill bit & drill ~ Wood glue ~ Satin spray varnish ~ DAP Fast n' Final spackle ~ Medium grit sandpaper ~ 1/4" plywood scrap ~ Paper punch ~ Glue gun

Assembly

Cut a hole in the side of the nipple gourd and place it on the top of the dipper gourd to form the head and glue. Place a gourd top on the backside of the dipper for the tail and glue. Cut two wings from scrap gourd and glue. When dry, apply spackle where the various pieces join the body. When dry, sand smooth.

Cut the boot tops from a cylindrical piece of gourd and the lowers from nearly flat gourd pieces. Place the bottoms in position on a plywood scrap and draw around them. Cut the plywood and glue the gourd bottoms to it. Glue the tops on and spackle if necessary. When dry, sand smooth.

Drill down through the center of each boot and glue the dowels in place. Slip the wood beads into place for the knees and glue. Mark where the dowels strike the bottom of the duck and drill two holes. Insert the dowels and glue.

The hat is just a gourd top. Cut earflaps from the watercolor paper and punch holes for the ribbons.

Painting the Piece

Use the wash brush to basecoat the entire duck White. Base the boots Green, the eye Black, and the beak Yellow.

Use the #12 and Pigskin to shade the beak and separate the upper and lower sections.

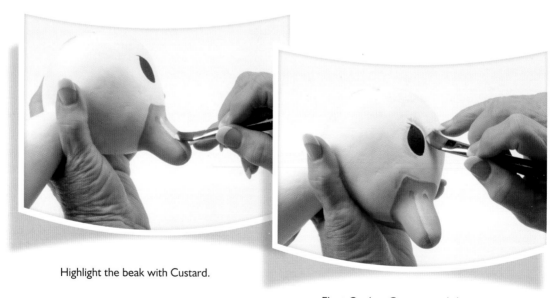

Highlight the beak with Custard.

Float Quaker Grey around the eyes and the corners of the mouth.

2 | T H E   P R O J E C T S

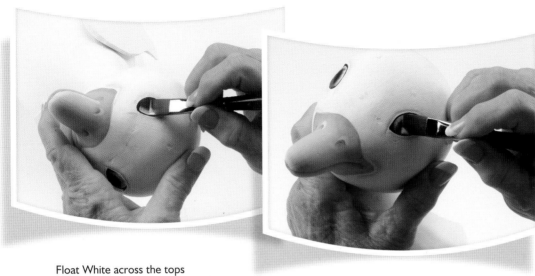

Float White across the tops of the eyes.

Float Yellow across the bottoms of the eyes. It may require more than one coat to show well.

Use the liner brush and White to add a comma strokes to the eyes for sparkle.

Paint the hat, ear-flaps, and ribbon Yellow. Hot glue the earflaps and the ribbons in the hat. Use the wood glue to put the hat on and tie the ribbons under his chin. Finish with several light coats of varnish, allowing drying time between coats.

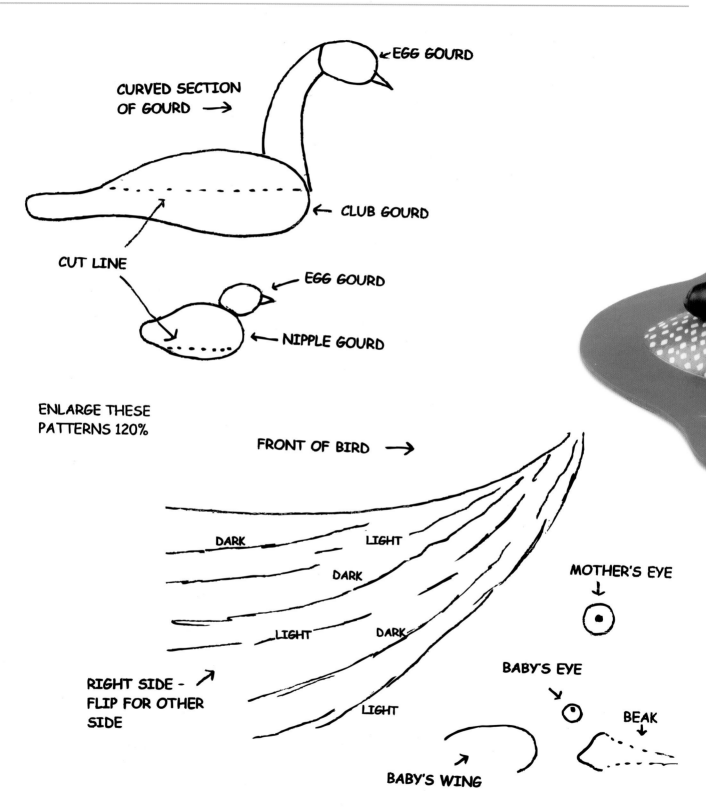

CURVED SECTION OF GOURD →

EGG GOURD

CLUB GOURD

CUT LINE

EGG GOURD

NIPPLE GOURD

ENLARGE THESE PATTERNS 120%

FRONT OF BIRD →

DARK

LIGHT

DARK

LIGHT

DARK

RIGHT SIDE - FLIP FOR OTHER SIDE

LIGHT

MOTHER'S EYE

BABY'S EYE

BEAK

BABY'S WING

Because of the unique nature of gourds, these patterns may have to be altered to fit each individual gourd. You may enlarge, shrink or alter them in any way necessary to make them work for you. To view over one hundred gourd patterns, visit her website TheFairyGourdmother.com.

Loon & Chick

PALETTE

Black ~ White ~ Moroccan Red ~ Charcoal ~ Denim Blue ~ Blue Mist ~ Navy Blue ~ Storm Grey ~ Adobe ~ Candy Bar Brown

BRUSHES

Series 7300 #2, 12 flat ~ Series 7350 10/0 liner ~ Series 7500 #2, 6 filberts ~ Series 7550 1" wash brush

SUPPLIES

Club gourd ~ Nipple gourd ~ 2 egg gourds ~ Snake gourd ~ DAP Fast n' Final spackle ~ Craft saw or knife ~ Wood glue ~ Fimo clay ~ Blending gel ~ 12" sq. Masonite ~ 3/16" dowel, 1" long ~ 3/16" dowel, 3" long ~ 3/16" drill bit & drill ~ Fine grit sandpaper

Assembly

The Mother Loon

Slice the side of the club gourd off after determining how high you want the Loon to ride in the water. Use the club with a rounded end rather than flat since it is the bird's breast.

Cut a portion of the snake for the neck and fit to the round end of the base. Make a hole in a large egg gourd and fit on the other end of the neck for the head. Drill a hole for the beak. Taper one end of the 3" dowel and glue in place. Mold clay around the dowel and form a point. Bake according to package directions.

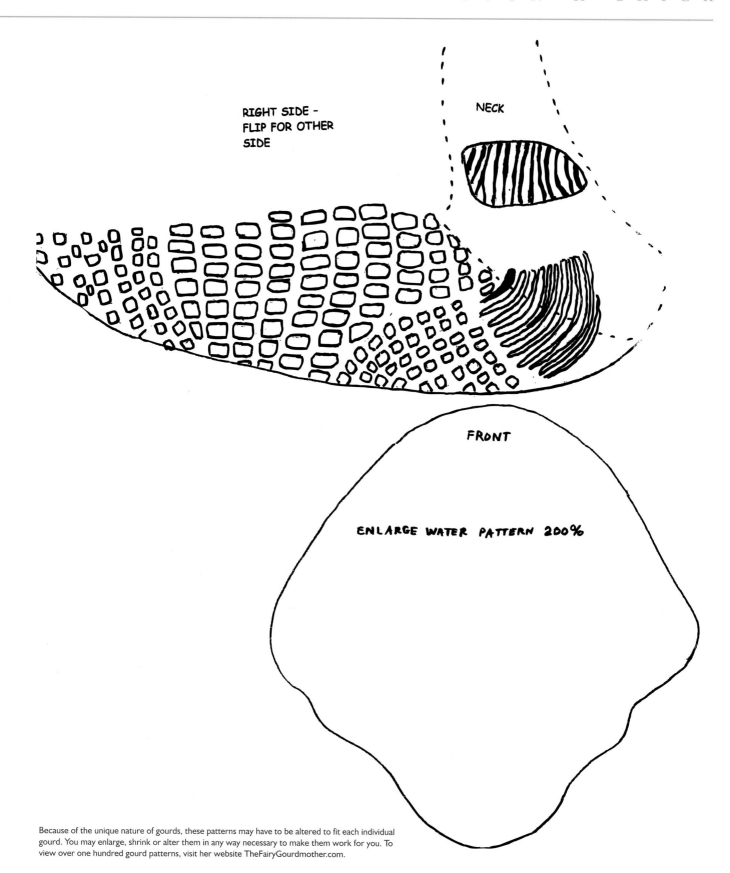

RIGHT SIDE –
FLIP FOR OTHER
SIDE

NECK

FRONT

ENLARGE WATER PATTERN 200%

Because of the unique nature of gourds, these patterns may have to be altered to fit each individual gourd. You may enlarge, shrink or alter them in any way necessary to make them work for you. To view over one hundred gourd patterns, visit her website TheFairyGourdmother.com.

The Loon Chick

Slice the side off a pointed nipple gourd as you did for the larger bird. Fit it to the back of the other bird. Slice a tiny bit off the small egg gourd to make the head fit snugly to the body and glue. Drill a hole in the head, taper one end of the 1" dowel and glue in place. Form the clay the same as for the large bird and bake.

Spackle all joints and sand smooth when dry. Do not join the two birds until they're painted.

Painting the Piece

The Mother Loon

Use the wash brush to coat the body with a mix of Storm Grey and White 3:1. Apply the pattern and paint the head and neck Black except for the White patch on the neck. Paint the breast White, the eyes Moroccan Red, and the beak Storm Grey.

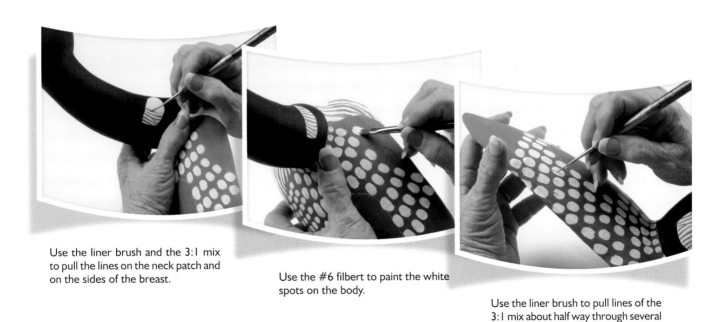

Use the liner brush and the 3:1 mix to pull the lines on the neck patch and on the sides of the breast.

Use the #6 filbert to paint the white spots on the body.

Use the liner brush to pull lines of the 3:1 mix about half way through several of the spots.

Use the #2 filbert brush to make the smaller dots near the back of the bird.

Use the liner brush to place white dots under the bird's chin.

Use the #12 flat brush to float Candy Bar Brown across the bottom of the eyes.

Paint the pupil Black.

Float across the top of the eyes with Adobe.

Place a White comma stroke in the same place in each eye.

Use the #12 flat to float the 3:1 mix around the eyes and then wash the area with Black to soften. If you can't maintain a thin Black line between the eye and the float, use the liner brush to make it.

Use a mix of Charcoal and White 2:1 and shade the beak.

The Loon Chick

Paint the chick Black and the breast White. Mop to soften where the two colors meet. Apply blending gel and tap in a mix of Charcoal and White 2:1 on the top portion of the white breast. Mop to soften.

Use the 2:1 mix to float around the eyes.

Use the stylus to place a White dot in the same place in each eye.

Use that same mix and the #12 flat to highlight the beak where it meets the head.

The same mix is used to float the wings.

The Water

Apply the pattern and cut off the excess Masonite. Use the 1" wash brush to basecoat with Denim Blue.

Apply blending gel and use the #12 flat and Blue Mist to float along the line on the side away from the bird's body.

Use the mop brush and pull strokes at an angle in one direction across the float. Repeat the mopping action and let dry.

Repeat the previous steps using Navy Blue and floating along the line on the side next to the body. Let dry.

Repeat the mopping action, pulling the mop across at an angle toward the body.

Use the liner brush and Blue Mist to pull wiggly lines down the center of the Blue Mist floats.

Use the Navy Blue to pull wiggly lines down the center of the Navy floats. Wash the entire surface with Denim.

Attach the chick to mother's back and attach the larger bird to the board. Fill any gaps between the two birds and between the mother and Masonite with spackle. When dry, touch up as needed. Finish with several light coats of spray varnish.

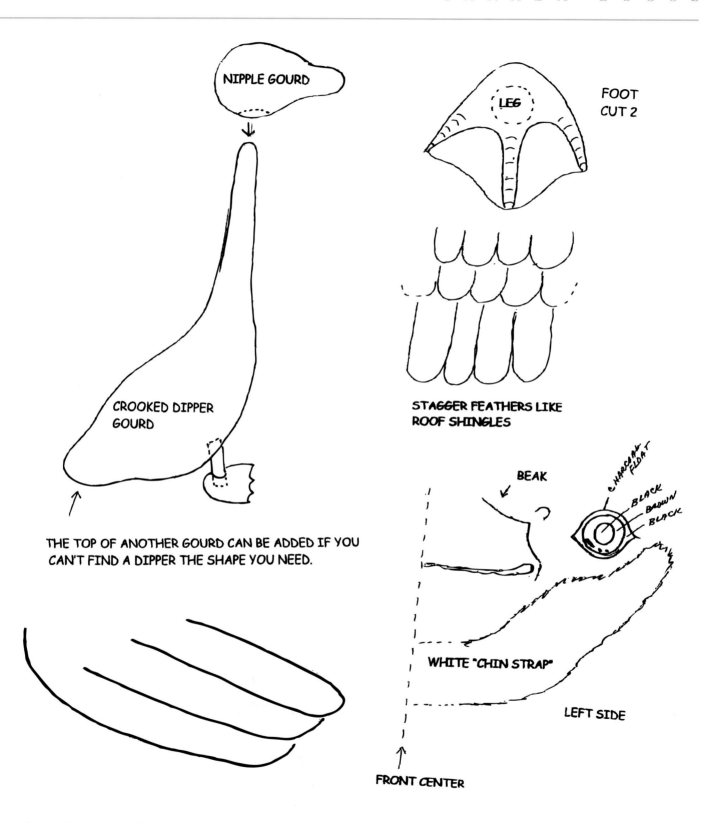

NIPPLE GOURD

FOOT
CUT 2

LEG

CROOKED DIPPER
GOURD

STAGGER FEATHERS LIKE
ROOF SHINGLES

THE TOP OF ANOTHER GOURD CAN BE ADDED IF YOU
CAN'T FIND A DIPPER THE SHAPE YOU NEED.

BEAK

CHARCOAL
FLOAT

BLACK
BROWN
BLACK

WHITE "CHIN STRAP"

LEFT SIDE

FRONT CENTER

Because of the unique nature of gourds, these patterns may have to be altered to fit each individual
gourd. You may enlarge, shrink or alter them in any way necessary to make them work for you. To
view over one hundred gourd patterns, visit her website TheFairyGourdmother.com.

Canada Goose

PALETTE

Black ~ White ~ Dark Burnt Umber ~ Brown Velvet Toffee ~ Hippo Grey ~ Brown Iron Oxide ~ Terra Cotta

BRUSHES

Series 7120 1/2" rake brush ~ Series 7300 #12 flat ~ Series 7350 10/0 liner ~ Series 7500 #6 filbert ~ Series 7550 1" wash brush

SUPPLIES

Nipple Gourd ~ Dipper gourd ~ Gourd pieces ~ DAP Fast n' Final spackle ~ Wood glue ~ Blending gel ~ Satin spray varnish ~ Craft saw or knife ~ Fine grit sandpaper

Assembly

Cut a hole in the side of the nipple gourd and fit it onto the top of the dipper gourd (see diagram). Cut the feet and legs from gourd pieces. Glue all pieces into place and let dry. Spackle all the joints and sand smooth when dry.

Painting the Piece

Use the wash brush to basecoat the head, beak, and neck Black. Paint the chin strap, chest, and the belly all the way to the tail with White. The back is Dark Burnt Umber and the feet and legs are Terra Cotta.

Apply blending gel to the lower chest, paint Dark Burnt Umber and quickly mop to soften. Be sure to keep the edges irregular where it meets the White. Leave the upper chest and rear end White.

Use the #12 and Hippo to float around the eyes and at the base of the beak. Also float a line to separate the upper and lower beaks. Leave a thin line of black between the float and the eye.

Also float around the nostrils with the same color.

Use the filbert and Brown Velvet for the eyes.

Paint the pupils Black.

Use the #12 to float a White c stroke across the top of each eye. Use the liner brush to place a White comma stroke in the same place in the eyes.

2 | T H E   P R O J E C T S

Use the liner brush and Toffee to make the feathers on the back and wings.

Use the rake brush and Dark Burnt Umber to pull lines across the Toffee markings to make them look striped.

A few of the wing feathers have back to back floats of Brown Iron Oxide. If the contrast is too harsh when you finish, wash the area with Dark Burnt Umber.

Use the #12 and Brown Iron Oxide to separate the webs on the feet and float lines on the legs. Finish with several light coats of spray varnish.

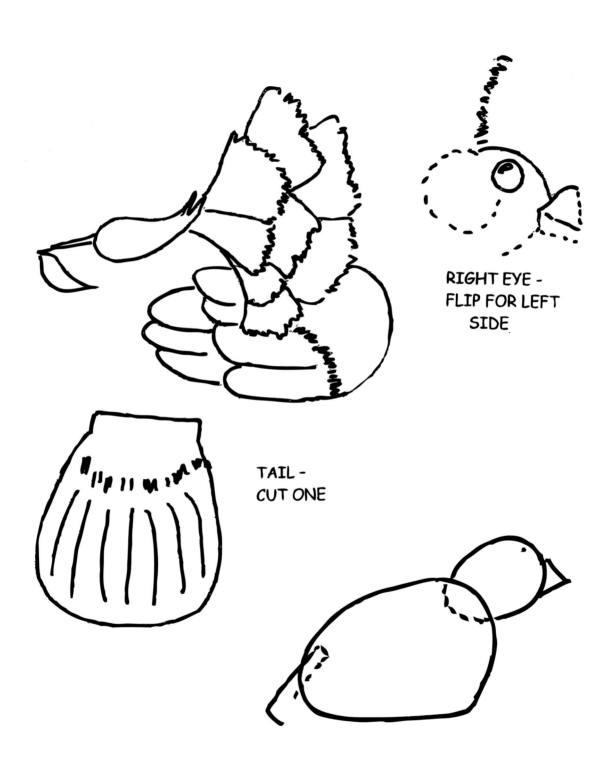

RIGHT EYE -
FLIP FOR LEFT
SIDE

TAIL -
CUT ONE

Because of the unique nature of gourds, these patterns may have to be altered to fit each individual gourd. You may enlarge, shrink or alter them in any way necessary to make them work for you. To view over one hundred gourd patterns, visit her website TheFairyGourdmother.com.

Goldfinch & Carnation

PALETTE

Opaque Yellow ~ Pale Yellow ~ Dark Goldenrod ~ Opaque Red ~ White ~ Dark Foliage ~ Medium Foliage

BRUSHES

Series 7300 #12 flat ~ Series 7350 10/0 liner ~ Series 7500 #4 filbert ~ Series 7520 1/2" filbert rake ~ Series 7550 1" wash brush ~ #6 sable brush

SUPPLIES

4-6" round gourd ~ Egg gourd ~ Gourd scraps ~ Fimo clay ~ DAP Fast n' Final spackle ~ Craft saw ~ Wood glue ~ Stylus ~ Satin spray varnish

Assembly

Find a gourd that is slightly off-center and sits sideways. Cut the egg gourd so that it fits snugly against the larger gourd. See the diagram. Cut the tail from a scrap and make a slot on the backside of the larger gourd. Angle the slot so that the tail doesn't stick straight out from the body. Glue in place and spackle the joint. When dry, sand smooth.

Form the beak from clay and use the stylus to make nostrils and scribe a line to separate the upper and lower beaks. Bake according to package directions. When cool, glue in place.

Painting the Piece

The Bird

Use the wash brush and Opaque Yellow to basecoat the bird. Use the rake brush and Dark Goldenrod to pull feathery lines all over the bird. Use the #12 and the same color for the beak.

Apply the pattern and paint the cap, eyes, tail, and lower wings Black. Use the rake brush to feather where the black meets the yellow.

Use the #12 to float a shadow of Dark Goldenrod around the wings and cheeks.

Use the liner brush and White to place a comma stroke in each eye.

Use the same brush and Pale Yellow to float a highlight on the inside of the wings and cheeks opposite the shadow.

Use the same brush and Pale Yellow to float a highlight on the inside of the wings and cheeks opposite the shadow.

Use the liner brush and White to place lines on the tail and wings.

Use the rake brush and Black to make the lines appear striped. Pull the strokes across the lines at an angle.

The Flower

Use the sable brush for this. Dress both sides of the brush with Opaque Red and then scoop a large amount of White on the back of the brush atop the red.

Set the brush down and apply pressure to fan the bristles. Rotate the brush between your fingers to further spread them.

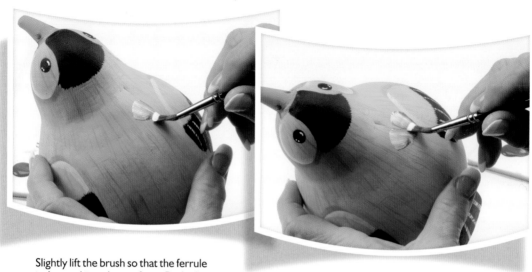

Slightly lift the brush so that the ferrule isn't touching the surface. Push the brush away from you just a little then pull it back. Rotate the handle and lift at the same time to bring the bristles back together.

Repeat this step reloading for each petal until you have an odd number of petals in the row. Drop down and add another row with two less petals than the previous row. It's best to have three rows — five, three, and one petals.

Turn the flower upside down. Use a dirty brush and load with the dark green on one side and the lighter green on the other side. Pull two strokes, tapering each one as you end.

Using the same brush, pull a thin line for the stem and then do a "sit-down" stroke for the leaves. Finish with several light coats of spray varnish.

Rubber Ducky

PALETTE

Yellow ~ White ~ Black ~ Pigskin ~ Poppy Orange ~ Tomato Spice

BRUSHES

Series 7300 #12 flat ~ Series 7350 10/0 liner ~ Series 7550 1" wash brush

SUPPLIES

Mexican bottle gourd 7-9" tall ~ Gourd scraps ~ DAP Fast n' Final spackle ~ Fine grit sandpaper ~ Wood glue ~ Spray varnish

Assembly

Cut the tops of scrap gourds to fit snugly against the bottle gourd for the bill and tail and glue in place. When dry, spackle the joints and let dry. Sand smooth.

RIGHT SIDE - FLIP
FOR LEFT SIDE

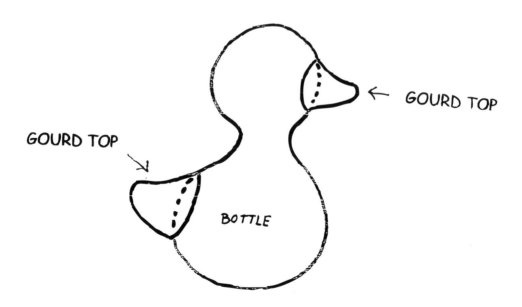

GOURD TOP

GOURD TOP

BOTTLE

Because of the unique nature of gourds, these patterns may have to be altered to fit each individual gourd. You may enlarge, shrink or alter them in any way necessary to make them work for you. To view over one hundred gourd patterns, visit her website TheFairyGourdmother.com.

Painting the Piece

Use the wash brush to undercoat the entire gourd White and then Yellow. Apply the beak and eye patterns. Basecoat the beak Poppy Orange and the eye White.

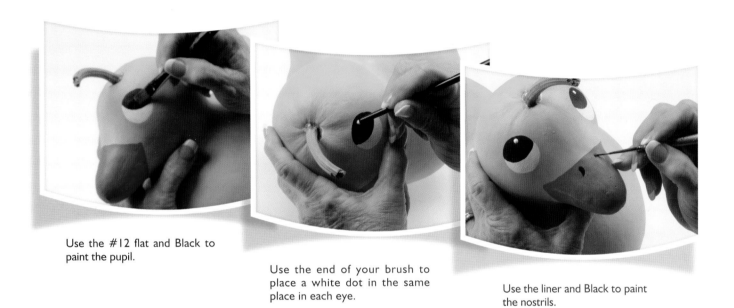

Use the #12 flat and Black to paint the pupil.

Use the end of your brush to place a white dot in the same place in each eye.

Use the liner and Black to paint the nostrils.

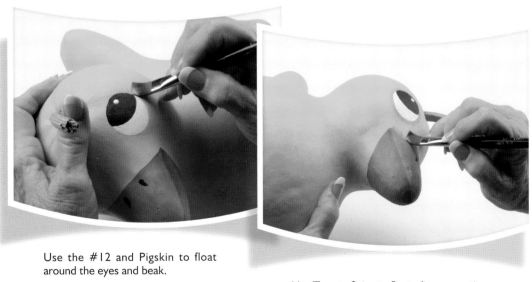

Use the #12 and Pigskin to float around the eyes and beak.

Use Tomato Spice to float a line separating the upper and lower beaks. Finish with several light coats of varnish.

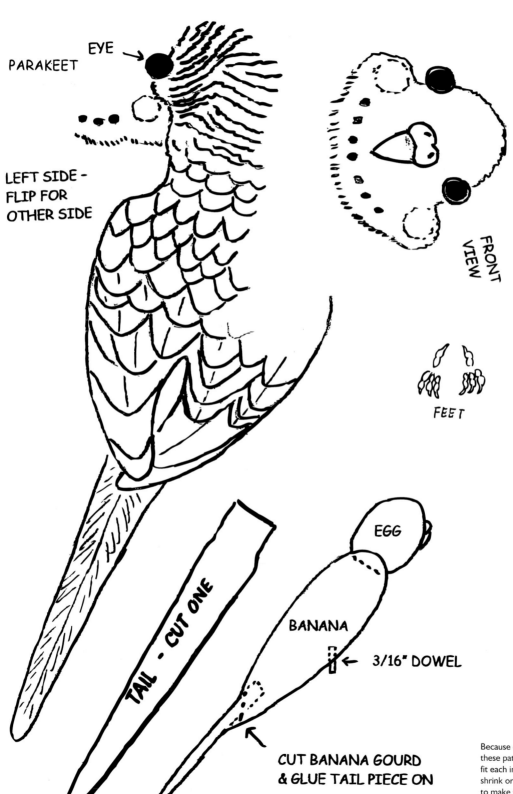

PARAKEET

EYE

LEFT SIDE -
FLIP FOR
OTHER SIDE

FRONT VIEW

FEET

TAIL - CUT ONE

EGG

BANANA

3/16" DOWEL

CUT BANANA GOURD
& GLUE TAIL PIECE ON

Because of the unique nature of gourds, these patterns may have to be altered to fit each individual gourd. You may enlarge, shrink or alter them in any way necessary to make them work for you. To view over one hundred gourd patterns, visit her website TheFairyGourdmother.com.

Parakeet

PALETTE

White ~ Black ~ Blue Mist ~ Rain Grey ~ Wedgewood Blue ~ Nightfall Blue ~ Storm Grey ~ Old Parchment

BRUSHES

Series 7300 #12 flat ~ Series 7350 10/0 liner ~ Series 7520 1/2" filbert rake

SUPPLIES

Banana gourd ~ Egg gourd ~ Gourd pieces ~ Fimo clay ~ DAP Fast n' Final spackle ~ Wood glue ~ Fine grit sandpaper ~ Craft saw ~ Stylus ~ Craft wire or hanger ~ 3/16" dowel, 1" long ~ 3/8" dowel, 4" long ~ 1/8", 3/8", 3/16" drill bits and drill ~ Short piece of rawhide thong ~ Satin spray varnish

Form a small piece of clay into a triangle and place on aluminum foil. Make two very small balls and apply to the top of the triangle. This should make the beak look heart-shaped. Smooth the joints and use the stylus to make nostrils. Bake according to package directions or about 10-11 minutes. When cool, glue on the bird.

Assembly

Cut a small portion of the egg gourd off so that it fits snugly on the large end of the banana gourd. Cut off the small curved end of the banana and cut a slot for the tail. Cut out the tail and glue in place. Spackle the joint and sand smooth when dry. Drill a 3/16" hole in the center of the 3/8" dowel and one in the bottom of the bird. Drill 1/8" holes in each end of the 3/8" dowel for the wire.

Painting the Piece

The Parakeet

Use the wash brush to basecoat the body Wedgewood Blue, the face and neck White, and the head and wings Black.

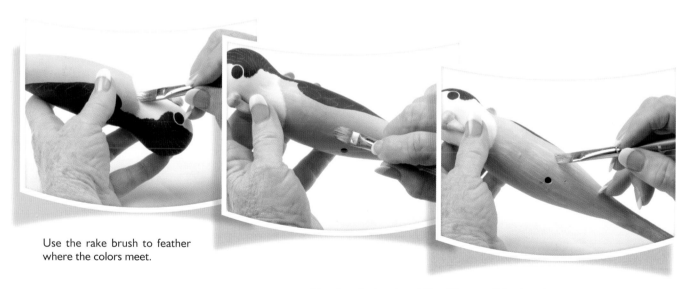

Use the rake brush to feather where the colors meet.

Use the rake brush and Blue Mist to pull feathery lines all over the blue portion of the bird.

2 | T H E   P R O J E C T S

Use the liner brush and White to outline the feathers
and to make the squiggly lines on the head.

Use the rake brush and Black to pull lines
across the white lines.

Use the # 12 and Nightfall to
float under the wings and around
the tail feathers.

Use the liner brush and Nightfall
to pull a vein down the center of
the main tail feather.

Use the corner of your brush and Wedgewood Blue to dab
in the cheeks and to paint the upper part of the nose.

Use Old Parchment to paint the lower
section of the nose. The two sections are
separate by a thin white line.

Use the liner and Black to
paint the "necklace."

Use the #12 and White to float across the top of the eye. Use
the liner brush to place a comma stroke across the bottom.

The Swing

Cut a length of coat hanger or piece of craft wire approximately 12-14" long. Using a piece of scrap wood, place nails in the configuration shown.

Bend the wire around the template. Then run the ends through the holes in the end of the perch.

Use pliers to bend the ends of the wire inward. Paint the perch white and glue the inch long dowel in place.

Use the liner brush and Rain Grey to paint the feet on the perch.

Shade the feet with Storm Grey. Glue bird to perch and finish with several light coats of spray varnish. Tie the thong on as a hanger.

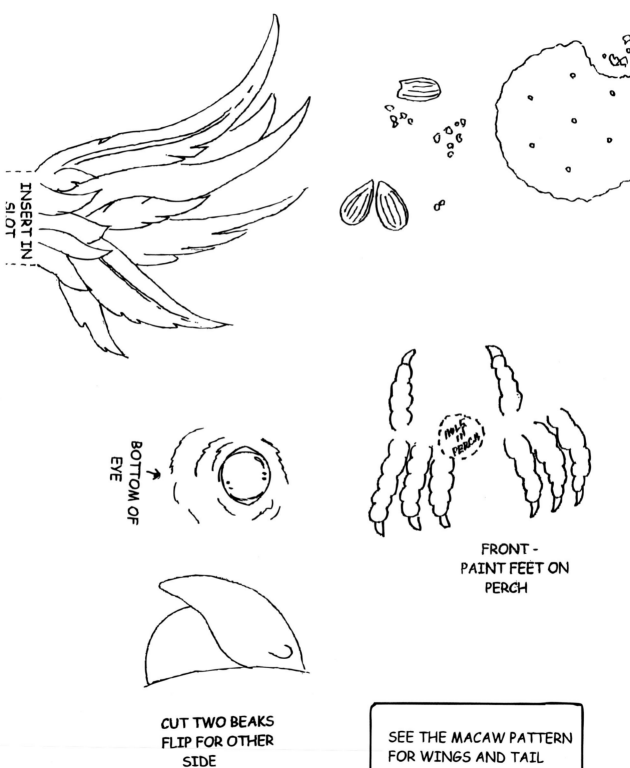

INSERT IN
SLOT

BOTTOM OF
EYE

FRONT -
PAINT FEET ON
PERCH

CUT TWO BEAKS
FLIP FOR OTHER
SIDE

SEE THE MACAW PATTERN
FOR WINGS AND TAIL

Because of the unique nature of gourds, these patterns may have to be altered to fit each individual
gourd. You may enlarge, shrink or alter them in any way necessary to make them work for you. To
view over one hundred gourd patterns, visit her website TheFairyGourdmother.com.

Sulphur-Crested Cockatoo

PALETTE

Storm Grey ~ Raw Sienna ~ Ivory ~ Drizzle Grey ~ White ~ Caribbean Blue ~ Rain Grey ~ Maple Sugar ~ Black ~ Brown Iron Oxide ~ Dolphin Grey ~ Custard ~ Opaque Yellow

BRUSHES

Series 7300 #12 flat ~ Series 7350 10/0 liner ~ Series 7550 1" wash brush

SUPPLIES

Bottle gourd, approx. 10" tall ~ Gourd pieces ~ 1" dowel, 6" long ~ Wood glue ~ Craft saw ~ 1/2" drill bit & drill ~ DAP Fast n' Final spackle ~ Fine grit sandpaper ~ 6" dia. wooden circle ~ 1/2" dowel, 12" long ~ 1/2" dowel, 1" long ~ Fimo clay ~ Satin spray varnish ~ Wood sealer

Assembly

Cut the wings, tail, and beak from the gourd pieces. Glue the beak together. It is only going to fit together on one plane. When the glue is dry, fill in the gaps with Fimo clay, fit to the face, and bake according to package directions. Do not attach the wings until they and the body are painted. Cut a slot for the tail and angle it slightly so that the tail can drop down in line with the body and doesn't stick straight out from the bird. Glue into place and, when dry, fill in where the two pieces meet with spackle. Sand smooth when dry. Drill 1/2" hole in the bottom of the bird, inset the 1" dowel halfway, and glue.

THE PERCH

Drill 1/2" hole all the way through the 1" dowel and in the center of the wooden circle. Insert the 12" dowel in the circle and glue. Place the 1" dowel halfway onto the 12" dowel, creating a "T" and glue. This leaves space for the dowel in the bird to fit into the 6" dowel later. Once the bird is finished, you will place it in that hole on the perch and glue — unless you prefer to leave it loose for ease of transportation.

Painting the Piece

Use the wash brush to basecoat the bird White. The beak and eyes are Black, and the crest is a mix of Custard and Raw Sienna 2:1.

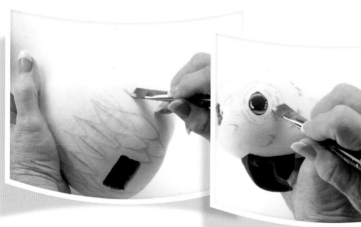

Use the #12 flat to shade around the feathers with Dolphin Grey and down each side of the veins. Notice how large the hole for the tail is. This is necessary to let the tail hand down. Make your hole a little at a time. You can always remove more, but it's very difficult to put it back.

Scatter Caribbean Blue accents throughout, especially around the eyes. Wash the entire piece with white if the shades seem too strong.

Float White "C" strokes in the corners of the eyes to make the eye appear round.

Use the liner brush to place white comma strokes and dots in each eye in the same place for highlight.

Use the #12 and Rain Grey to separate the two parts of the beak. Also float around the nostrils.

Shade the crest with Raw Sienna. Also float down each side of the veins in the feathers.

Deepen a few of the shadows with Brown Iron Oxide.

Highlight the crest with Opaque Yellow.

Tip some of the feathers with White.

Use the liner brush to highlight the veins with Opaque Yellow.

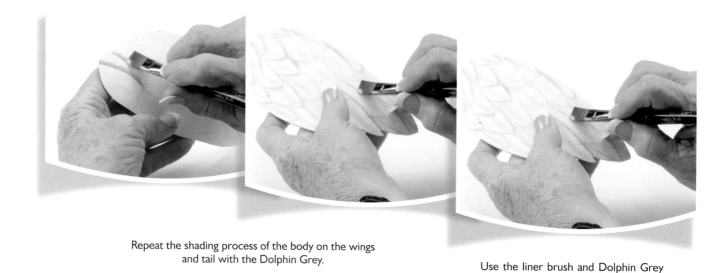

Repeat the shading process of the body on the wings and tail with the Dolphin Grey.

Use the liner brush and Dolphin Grey to make small splits in some of the wing and tail feathers.

The Perch

Use the wash brush to paint the base Story Grey. Apply the pattern and paint the cracker and crumbs Maple Sugar, the seeds Drizzle Grey, and the feet Rain Grey.

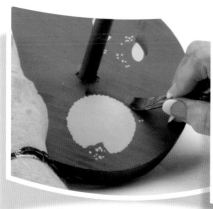

Use the #12 and Black to shade around one side of the cracker and seeds.

Shade the cracker with Raw Sienna. Randomly touch in small patches of Raw Sienna all over the cracker.

Quickly mop to soften the patches.

2 | T H E   P R O J E C T S

Use the stylus to place the Black holes in the cracker.

Highlight around one side of the holes and touch in small patches of Ivory. Mop again to soften the patches.

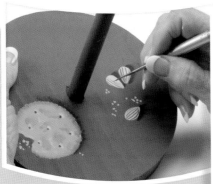

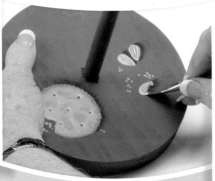

Use the liner and Rain Grey to paint the stripes on the seeds.

Float a highlight of White on the seeds on the side opposite the shadow.

Shade around one side of the feet.

When all of the pieces are painted, glue the wings on the bird. Finish with several light coats of varnish.

Shade the feet with Storm Grey.

Highlight the feet with Drizzle Grey.

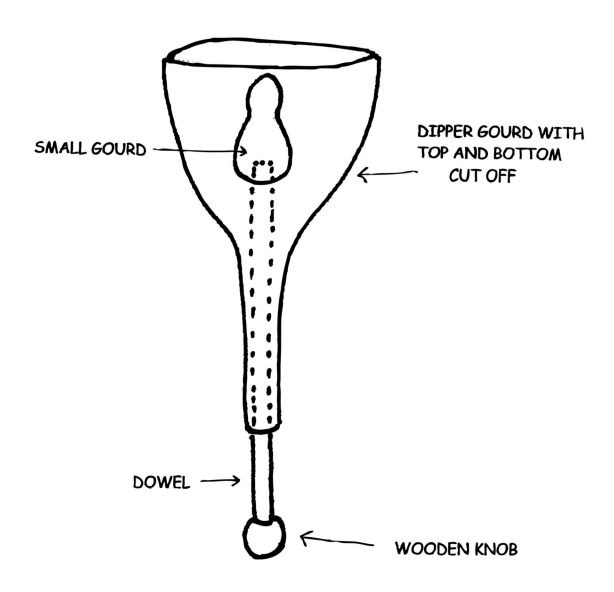

SMALL GOURD

DIPPER GOURD WITH TOP AND BOTTOM CUT OFF

DOWEL

WOODEN KNOB

Because of the unique nature of gourds, these patterns may have to be altered to fit each individual gourd. You may enlarge, shrink or alter them in any way necessary to make them work for you. To view over one hundred gourd patterns, visit her website TheFairyGourdmother.com.

Birdie Pop-Up Toy

PALETTE

Dark Foliage ~ Light Foliage ~ Spice Tan ~ Spice Brown ~ Flesh Tan ~ White ~ Black ~ Antique Gold ~ Burnt Sienna ~ Opaque Red ~ Black Cherry

BRUSHES

Series 7000 #6 round ~ Series 7300 #12 flat ~ Series 7350 10/0 liner

SUPPLIES

Dipper gourd ~ Nipple gourd ~ 1/2" dowel, approx. 12" long ~ 1/2" drill bit & drill ~ Craft saw ~ 1 1/4" wooden knob with 1/2" hole ~ Small grapevine wreath ~ White boa ~ Sea sponge ~ Wood glue ~ Hot glue gun ~ Satin spray varnish

Assembly

Cut the bulb portion of the dipper in half, per the diagram. Cut off an inch or two of the handle end. Clean the gourd out and use the dowel to clear the handle. Drill a hole in the bottom of the nipple gourd, and glue the knob to the dowel.

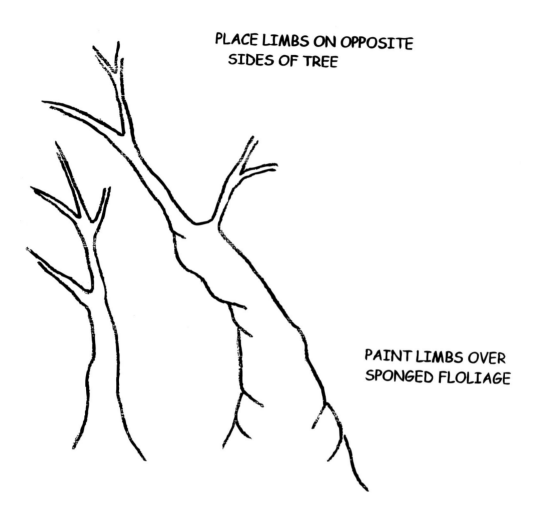

PLACE LIMBS ON OPPOSITE
SIDES OF TREE

PAINT LIMBS OVER
SPONGED FLOLIAGE

SIDE VIEW
OF BIRD

TOP VIEW
OF BIRD

Because of the unique nature of gourds, these patterns may have to be altered to fit each individual gourd. You may enlarge, shrink or alter them in any way necessary to make them work for you. To view over one hundred gourd patterns, visit her website TheFairyGourdmother.com.

Painting the Piece

The Dowel

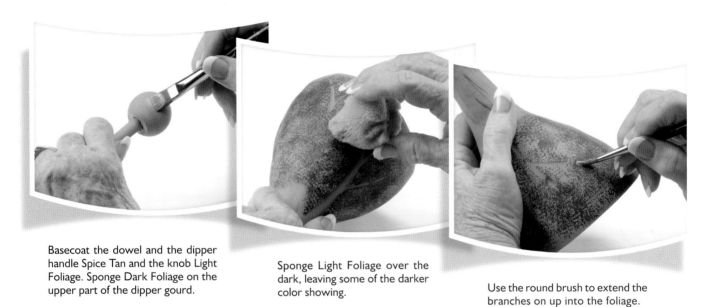

Basecoat the dowel and the dipper handle Spice Tan and the knob Light Foliage. Sponge Dark Foliage on the upper part of the dipper gourd.

Sponge Light Foliage over the dark, leaving some of the darker color showing.

Use the round brush to extend the branches on up into the foliage.

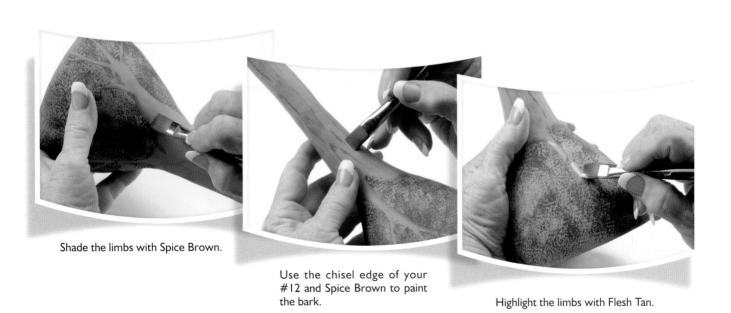

Shade the limbs with Spice Brown.

Use the chisel edge of your #12 and Spice Brown to paint the bark.

Highlight the limbs with Flesh Tan.

The Birdie

Paint the nipple gourd Opaque Red, the beak Antique Gold, and the eye Black. Float White in each corner of the eye to make it appear round.

Use the liner brush and White to place a comma stroke in the same place in each eye.

Float Burnt Sienna inside the beak, leaving a gold margin.

Float Spice Brown over the Burnt Sienna on the upper beak only and then use the liner brush and Black to paint a thin line along the edge of the Spice Brown.

Touch a bit of White to the upper beak for highlight.

Float the wings with Black Cherry. Finish with several light coats of varnish.

Putting Birdie on the Dowel

Place hot glue around the inside of the gourd.

Glue the boa in place and then place glue on the end of the dowel and glue the bird on.

Glue the grapevine wreath in place. You may have to unwind and rewind the wreath to make it fit the top of your gourd. I soaked mine to make it easier to work with. Enjoy your toy!

GALLERY

GALLERY

GALLERY

G A L L E R Y

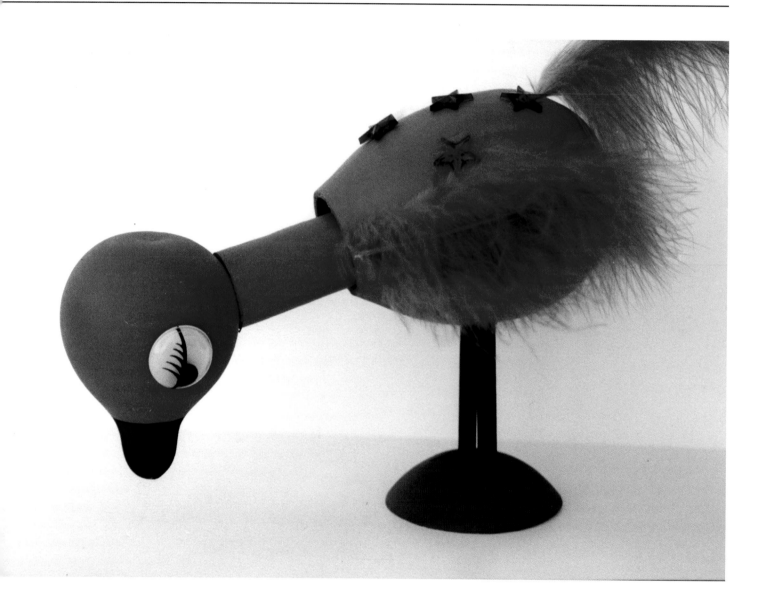

GALLERY

The gourds used in this book came from PumpkinHollow.com and Dalton Farms, 610 CR 336, Piggott, AR 72454; you can contact them through e-mail at ddalton@piggott.net or call 870-598-3568. All paints are Delta Ceramcoat and the brushes are Loew-Cornell.

Tom Keller

P.O. Box 1115

West Point, MS 39773

www.new.enterit.com/Tom3334

662-494-3334

Fern Sink Farm

14371 NW 50 Avenue

Chiefland, FL 32626

fernsinkfarm.com

352-493-2327

Blessings Farm

475 Chapel Church Road

Red Lion, PA 17356

blessingsfarms.com

(toll free) 877-638-0644

Welburn Farms

40635 De Luz Road

Fallbrook, CA 92028

welburngourds.com

(toll free) 877-420-2613

Foothill Farms

11341 Eddyburg Road

Newark, OH 43055

foothillsfarms.com

(toll free) 877-346-8445